CW00863146

PERCEPTION IS REALITY

"Reality is merely an illusion,
albeit a very persistent one."
- A. Einstein

Perception is Reality

You are not allowed to succeed.

You are not good enough to succeed.

If you're like most people, this statement is repeated with depressing regularity, like a self-determining echo. That echo pounds like a mighty war drum, sounding the steady march towards a miserable life full of heartache, mediocrity, and eternal frustration. By the mere act of repetition, you force it to become true to you.

A perceived truth is reality.

Meaning, what you believe to be true – IS true, until you believe otherwise.

In a world FILLED with confirmation bias, it is disparagingly true that folks like you and I are getting more entrenched in our bunkers of belief, and less willing to have a truly open mind – ready and willing to accept new truths.

This is unfortunate as it tends to make us victims of our perception if we cannot break the trends of stubborn dogma.

The greatest gift that the universe could ever possibly give you is the understanding of just how malleable and transformable your perception really is.

You alone create your perception; therefore you alone determine your reality. If you choose to always be "stuck", you will always BE stuck – until you choose freedom. If you simply CHOOSE freedom – the amazing thing is – no shackle, no prison, no person can entrap you. You are truly free, the very moment you decide that you are.

In life, as you know – no matter how hard we try – we simply cannot control all of the events that happen around us. No matter how hard you try, no matter the methods or tactics you employ. You may be able to control some of them, but eventually — some uncontrollable, unforeseeable event takes place. Chaos theory. Murphy 's Law.

Do not let this discourage you.

This is exactly where you take control of your destiny.

This is exactly where you take control of your life.

This is where you realize that, although you may not be able to control external forces, stimuli, or people – you CAN control your REACTION to it.

By controlling your reaction – you create untold power. This is a power that most people never harness. This is a power that most people never even REALIZE is possible for them to control.

You can control your thoughts. You can control your words. You can control your actions, and your reactions.

A very simple phrase to carry with you, one that my mentor taught to me years ago, is this:

"Control your words, control your thoughts, control your actions."

It is in this order for a reason. By controlling your words – you create a hypnotic state in your subconscious. You control your 'input' and your 'output' simultaneously.

One thing you will notice as a stark difference between successful people and those who are miserable is the words that they use.

The successful master their diction. The words they use are more precise, and they are more positive. You seldom hear a successful person using words like "lose", "fail", "should", "can't" and a myriad of other negatively impacting words. They avoid the use of these words for a reason. These negative word choices impact your thoughts, your emotions, your surroundings, and those who grace your social circle.

Miserable people tend to use a lot of self-pity in their speech. "It's not fair", "It's not my fault", "You just don't understand MY situation", "No", "I can't", "I should", "I'm a failure" and many more.

If you hear that shit every day, or even a couple times a week – it starts to create a disability. It creates impairment.

The longer you continue with these negative word patterns – the harder it seems to be to change. The harder it seems to speak consistently positively, and the harder it seems to hold yourself accountable.

Nobody is going to save you, except yourself.

To master your words, I highly suggest an exercise of placing an elastic band on your wrist. EVERY time you use a negative language pattern, I want you to pull that elastic back and SNAP your wrist as hard as you can. This creates a pattern interrupt, and creates a synaptic crossfire in your brain (fancy words for "it starts breaking a bad habit").

Once you've snapped yourself, it doesn't end there. Correct your negative language pattern with one that is enabling, empowering, and positive. We'll talk more on that a little later.

As an example – my wife Erika is a wild-mustang horse trainer. Sometimes, when she is training a particularly stubborn horse, she will say something to the effect of, "I don't think I'm going to do well with this horse!"

To which, I reply – "Change your words to something like: 'this is tough, but I know we'll exceed my expectations by putting in a consistent effort with a focused goal in mind'."

Once she makes this tiny shift – her training of that particular horse often improves dramatically. Then they kick butt at their horse competitons.

Funny how that works, isn't it?

Mastering your thoughts is the easy task.

All you need to do is change your input. By changing your input – I am simply saying – read books, take courses, watch videos on YouTube or elsewhere on the internet. Make sure that this material is positive, constructive, and helps you attain your goals of a positive, useful mindset.

As a bonus to you for purchasing this book – I have created a list of successful, positive people, channels, and ideas to follow on the internet.

You can find them by going to the following webpage: readshanehunter.com/success-list

If you follow these positive examples for a minimum of 30 days, your mindset will be completely different. Obviously the longer that you immerse yourself in this training each day, the faster and the stronger your results will be. I've been going strong now for 5+ years, and it's worked well for me.

To change your actions, you're already 2/3 of the way there if you follow the last 2 steps to change your words, and your thoughts. Your actions tend to follow your words and your thoughts.

However, if you are REALLY stubborn like me, then I suggest you employ the very same elastic band trick I showed you for controlling your words (hint: you can also use that trick for negative thoughts).

Anytime you find yourself engaging in self-sabotage, self-destruction, or really any particular activity that doesn't move you forward as a person, and towards the success that you crave – then you need to break the pattern, & change your destiny.

You can change things like getting drunk or high to going and working out. The endorphins you release during working out will give you a state change, without the hangover – plus there are long-term health benefits, and you'll look a whole lot better too.

You can change from spending your money frivolously on entertainment, eating out, or other fleeting things – into a time for reflection. Imagine, if you saved that money – and spent that time setting some awesome goals. Maybe a dream trip to a destination that you've always wanted to visit or going to a seminar and learning some skills that you've always wanted to have. How much more powerful would THAT be than another lunch at McDonalds, or seeing the latest movie?

When you're creating these substitutions, think about the process that led you to engage in the negative behavior. Think about alternative courses of action that could lead you to better decisions.

Remove patterns from your life that are money or time thieves. We generally take on these habits to avoid dealing with real life, and to 'escape'. If you plan your escapes – they are a heck of a lot better. I promise.

Meditate on these things – and you will be amazed at how dramatically your life will change for the better.

It will seem difficult at first.

It IS difficult at first.

I know. I've been there. Every now and then (honestly – way more than I'd like to admit), I still act, think, or speak impulsively. Every day new challenges arise. Every day new opportunities abound internally, and externally.

Rest assured, my friend - with enough time, practice, and discipline – this mastery will be yours.

The knowledge contained in the upcoming chapters will enable you to master these most valuable success strategies.

It is my sincere hope that you will take action on them immediately. Simply reading them, and not doing anything with this knowledge will get you no further. In fact, I'd consider that – wasting your time.

So it is time to commit.

Commit not only to reading this book, but to taking action on the words in this book – however you deem fit.

Knowledge is powerful.

Applied knowledge is **POWER**.

This is my bold, yet honest promise to you.

When you read this entire book, and actively apply its principles – if you don't see dramatic results and immediate changes in your life,send the book to me, and I will refund your money. I don't know of any other book, or any other author making such a guarantee.

So... Let's get started. Shall we?

II

PERMISSION & VALIDATION

"What the superior man seeks is in himself;
what the small man seeks is in others."
                                    - Confucious

Permission and Validation

"Shane! Whatever you do, do NOT touch this iron! It is VERY hot, and it will burn you," my mother said one day, as we stood in our basement laundry room.

What is hot? What does 'burn me' mean? I thought to myself, in semi-obedient silence.

Just like that, almost as quickly as my mother turned around to fold some of the laundry, I quickly reached for the iron, and stuck my index finger on the shiny metal bottom of the red hot iron.

"OWWWWWWWWWWWW!!" I yelled in pain.

"Did you touch the iron???" my mother asked me, spinning around with the seemingly gale force of a hurricane.

"Yes…" I cried out.

"What did I tell you? When I tell you things, it's for your own good! I'm trying to keep you safe. You need to listen to me! You need to ask permission before you do things, or stuff LIKE THIS will happen!" my mother replied kindly, albeit with a look of obvious irritation painted upon her face.

That's my first memory of being taught that I need permission to do something – otherwise there would be pain involved. MASSIVE pain.

I was 4 years old, but I remember it to this day like it was yesterday.

From the time that you became conscious as a wee lad or lass, you have been indoctrinated with a concept that has altered your life – without you even knowing it.

Your parents, your extended family, your teachers, hell… society as a whole has beat into your head that you need permission, and you need validation before you are able to commit to any thought, to any action, or to speak out with what is on your heart and mind.

Permission needs to be granted from an early age to do anything, from:

- Going outside
- Playing with certain friends
- Choosing your own meals
- Choosing your own clothing
- Etc., etc., etc...

Permission needs to be granted even in adulthood for things like:

- When to show up for work, and when you can go home
- What to take in college
- What hobbies to pursue

It doesn't SEEM like a big deal, and there is really nothing WRONG with this. Permission tends to keep us safe when we are incapable of making our own decisions. These decisions can mean life or death, and these decisions can shape our future. Permission guides our decisions. Who guides our permission?

Do you want to achieve *more* from life than those who have decided your fate thus far?

What happens when you're old enough to make your own decisions?

Eventually, I believe that you become capable of determining right from wrong, good from bad, and positive from negative. As such, the true need for permission dissolves, yet the subconscious need for permission remains clear and distinct - like trying to mix oil and water.

Our parents, teachers, and society try their hardest to accommodate this fact, some earlier than others. They tend to replace "giving you permission" with "giving you validation".

They allow you to make your own decisions, then they reinforce your good decisions with affirmation (or "validation"), and reprimand your bad decisions with disappointment (a lack of "validation").

When I was younger, my parents placed me in several martial arts programs – from Karate to Tae-Kwon-Do. For some reason I had a tendency to kick ass in martial arts. I was always at the top of my class. I attribute this mostly to my obsession with all things fighting – from Bruce Lee, Jean-Claude Van Damme, and Chuck Norris movies to professional wrestling.

Anyway… in martial arts – when you increase your skill level enough – you are tested, and if you pass said test – granted a new belt that is a new color.

This tradition symbolizes the mastery of the art, science, skills, and understanding that is required of each martial art.

Whenever I would take my tests, I remember being so nervous and anxious every time as I waited for my test to begin . When the test was actually happening – I was completely 'in the zone', and performed on an almost subconscious level.

When the test was over, and I was handed my new belt in the ceremony – my instructor and the league judges would congratulate me, they would tell me how well I had done. They would validate me.

It made me feel amazing. Really, it made me feel better than amazing. It was the best feeling in the world. I craved it. I needed it. I felt incomplete without it.

I also remember, later on at more advanced stages – when I didn't quite pass my test – and being told that I had failed. I remember the pain, the heartache, the almost complete depression of disappointing my instructor, my parents, and myself. The lack of validation was devastating.

Thankfully, I understood that it wasn't the end when I didn't pass. It just meant I needed to work harder, and think more about what I was doing until, like earlier tests, it became subconscious mastery.

I never again wanted to be in this situation. I only wanted the success. It was bigger than getting a different colored belt. The success I found – was discovered in my triumph over the need for validation. It no longer drove me.

External validation no longer mattered to me. The only thing that mattered was working hard on advancement – for the sake of getting better – on both a conscious and a subconscious level.

When I stopped focusing on my need for validation, and started completely focusing on the task at hand, and becoming the best at what I was doing – this is where I truly started advancing more quickly than I ever had before.

We tend to learn to seek out validation, wherever and whenever we can find it. Our ego demands it.

We seek validation before we act.

We seek validation after we act.

We also learn to fear disapproval & disappointment.

We learn to avoid a lack of validation.

So, as you can now see, from a very early age every single decision we make, every action we take is subconsciously affected by a need for permission and/or a need for validation.

The fact that your subconscious mind holds on to these perceived 'needs' into adulthood –

may just be a portion of what is holding YOU back from achieving success, and happiness.

The next time you decide that you want to make a big decision – try to analyze what's going on in the inner workings of your mind. I am completely certain that you will find that there is a nagging need for permission or for validation.

There is an 'iffyness' about truly committing to the decision. You may not be quite sure why you are unable to be 100% certain. You just can't place your finger on it…

There is a very good chance that it's because without that permission or validation – your decision seems incomplete.

Something seems to be missing.

The question is – now that we have established that this requirement for permission or validation exists – what can we possibly DO about it?

The answer is found within your personality type...

The options are:

1. You can decide that from this moment forward you no longer *require* permission or validation to think, speak, and do anything that you want to do.

2. You can decide that from this moment forward that you hereby grant yourself universal, unequivocal, unrestrained permission or validation to think, speak, and do anything that you want to do. You now have permission AND validation for anything your heart desires. Forever. If you can't grant it to yourself – you at least have both permission and validation from me. So that's one. One is definitely better than none, use that momentum and move forward into the life you deserve.

Either choice means permanently saying goodbye to the subliminal requirements that are currently restraining you and keeping you from greatness.

Either choice requires the commitment to the understanding that you alone decide your own future.

You decide what is right or wrong, negative and positive.

You decide your future.

You decide your fate.

Either choice means you no longer let anyone else control the shape of your future, the scope of your success, or the strength of your happiness.

Either choice means you are now free.

You do as you please, when you please, and how you please.

You think the thoughts of your choosing.

You speak with the words that you hold to be most true.

You walk with integrity – knowing that your words, your thoughts and your actions are congruent, and they are coming from you, not anybody else.

It's a great responsibility that you are taking on, eclipsed only by the greatness of the freedom that is now laid before you.

I used to let other people's opinions bother me, and guide my decisions – then I realized, other people's opinions neither paid my bills, nor did they get me any closer to what I wanted in life.

What has the need for permission or the need for validation been keeping you from?

What are you going to do with your newfound freedom from the need for validation or permission?

III

CAN I SEE YOUR ID, PLEASE?

"Man know thyself;
then thou shalt know the Universe and God."
- Pythagoras

SELF-ESTEEM

Guaranteed to make you
think at least twice as
highly of yourself.

Caution: Overdose can
have negative side effects.

30 tablets

Can I See Your ID, Please?

You can be anyone you want to be, and still be yourself.

Your ID is yours to define.

You will need to let go of some people, and bring in new people. Just realize, this is not an inherently good or bad thing – it simply "is".

People are meant for seasons in our lives. Some last longer than others. Some last longer that we'd like them to. Others last for what seems a mere blink – and then they're gone, all too soon.

Don't fear it; embrace it for what it is. Every interaction moves you further ahead and helps lead you to where you need to be.

Before you can effectively define your ID, you're going to need to answer five critical questions:

Who is it that you want to be?

Who are you now?

What needs to happen to get from who I am now, to who I want to be?

Is my current social circle supplemental in my transition to who I want to be?

Who can I bring into my social circle that can and will help me become closer to the "me" I seek?

To find out whom it is that you want to be – grab a pen and some paper, and put on your proverbial "thinking cap". Think about all the people that you love, think about the things you've always wanted to do, and the places you've wanted to go. Write all that down.

Define your perfect day, on paper - down to every last detail. Describe what the weather is like, what the surrounding area looks like. Write down who is with you, what you're wearing, how you're feeling, what you do during the course of that day. What conversations do you have? What meals do you eat? What events fill your day? How do you interact with people? Answer these questions, and any other questions you can think of and you'll be well on your way to defining "future you".

Figuring out who you are now is fairly simple. Just like above, write everything down – only this time, instead of writing down your "ideal day", write down what you honestly do each day. Be detailed. How are you with people? What is your general mood? What do you want from life? Why do you want it?

What do you need to do to get yourself from who you are now – to who you want to be? Are there bad habits, not enough money, not enough time – what is it? What is missing? Figure that out, and write it down. Do NOT let this overwhelm you – it's all a part of a proven process, and you will get there. All you need to do is simply follow the steps.

Who is currently in your social circle? Who are your friends? Who are your co-workers / bosses / employees? Who are your family members that you interact with most? Who are 'random' people that you tend to see every day? Write them down, and write down the effect that you feel they have on your life. Why do they have that effect? Can you change that effect immediately? Are they bad apples who would rather see you down in the gutter with them, or would they want to see you uplifted and edified?

Who do you know that is living the life that you desire? Who do you know that is at the very least, "closer" to living the life that you desire most? How can you meet more people who have what you want, and that are willing to help you get there? What investments (time or money) can I make to fast-track my networking with these individuals or groups? If you have more money than time, use the money to get into mastermind groups, exclusive clubs, etc. If you have more time than money – maybe you can help those that have what you want, in some way that they need help. Every little bit helps, just do everything with intention – and give value back. For these folks to like you – you can't just 'take'; you will need to give back. Find a way to do this and you will find yourself surrounded by the exact people that you need to be around to make your dreams a reality.

When you find yourself in tough situations, try asking yourself and envisioning – *how would these role models of mine handle this situation?*

Take what you wrote down about who you currently are, combined with who you want to be, and the list / attributes of your current social circle. Ask your newfound mentors how they would go about transitioning from who you are to who you want to be. Ask them for advice on your current social circle.

Picture yourself as 'future you'. What does current you need to do to get there? You'll be surprised at how quickly answers will start to pour in, after you've thought on this for a while.

Start believing that you are now 'future you'. Feel, think, speak, and act like you would assume 'future you' would, make a habit of it. Create a powerful new self-image. Don't worry if you stumble – this process is just like learning how to ride a bicycle. It's merely practice. It doesn't matter how many times you fall off.

The only thing that matters, is that you learn to ride the bike – or in this case, that you learn to BE 'future you'.

Author and speaker, Tony Robbins states that most self-sabotage occurs when we fall out of line with what our self-image is.

If you think and believe that you are a failure – you will remain a failure.

If you think and believe that you will always remain poor – you will remain poor.

If you see yourself undeserving of a brilliant and encouraging social circle – you will keep a social circle that is neither brilliant, nor encouraging.

If you think, speak, and act like you want to become... Guess what? That's *exactly* what you will become.

What do you think makes lottery winners go bankrupt within a few short years?

Aside from the obvious issue of not knowing how to handle their money, it comes from an even deeper rooted problem. They never saw themselves as a wealthy person – they instead saw themselves as lucky, and undeserving of the newfound wealth.

So POOF!

Just like magic, they fall back into insolvency.

Instead of seeing themselves as who they now are – and adapting to it by learning money management and investing skills – they go out and buy expensive houses, Lamborghinis and hookers and blow for all their closest friends. The same friends who weren't so close before the money...

As a result, they are left with no friends and no money. They're back to square one.

A few years ago, I was a server / waiter at a restaurant called Applebee's. I was great at it, but that was the pinnacle of my professional career until that point.

27-28 years old – and I was still at the same type of job that I'd had 10 years before. No ambitions of climbing the corporate ladder – that thought repulsed me.

I wasn't miserable per se, as I was making decent money (like $200-$300 / 6 hour shift). I had great friends who served and bartended with me. There really wasn't much incentive to move up, or on.

Yet, there in the back of my mind... There was a nagging... An aching desire for more from life...

That pain motivated me to seek change...

After reading hundreds of books (literally), pouring through courses and videos on self-development and skill development in the field of marketing – with an emphasis on internet marketing – I all of a sudden had a new – highly valuable skill set.

I knew multiple ways to bring companies of any size, in any industry; ample numbers of leads, lots of customers, and in turn – lots of money.

My consultancy started with a bang – my first client was paying me $10,000 / month for reputation management.

I used the profits from that gig to scale up my business. I hired a professional copywriter and a professional web designer – and took my online presence to the next level.

Within just 3 or 4 short months I was generating an income of well over $35,000 / month and had 2 employees (I hired and trained 2 of my good friends).

We were living 3 blocks from the beach in sunny Encinitas, California. We were hitting the gym daily with a personal trainer. We were eating at Ruth's Chris Steakhouse – taking monthly trips to Vegas and staying in some ridiculous suites. Disneyland happened at least once a week, and tons of other vacations.

We had gone from living with my wife's parents in her old bedroom just a year before – struggling & depressed to be barely scraping by. We were working so hard at paying off our massive debt load and then one day, at the height of my consultancy I was earning in excess of $35K a month. We were seldom bored. We were living the dream.

Or, so we thought…

With all of this success – entirely too much stress for me to handle at the time crept up, and broadsided me like a baseball bat to the side of the head.

I wasn't ready for the levels of success that I had found.

So what happened next?

Well...

My skills were there. The value I offered my customers was quite obviously there also. My ambition was at an all-time high. I outworked my employees – I outworked everybody I knew. I was driven harder than a rally car approaching the finish line in a neck and neck race.

Yet, one thing lacked.

A clear and concise image of who I was, and who I wanted to be was not present.

See, the only thing I had focused on for the previous two years – was that I wanted to be rich. I wanted to make more money than anyone I knew.

I wanted to do it by helping people. Good people; people who were trying to make a difference, people who were job creators, people who were hard working employees, good folks who simply wanted more from life.

In an economy full of negativity – I was looking to create positivity all around me. I wanted that positivity to spread like a virus.

It's funny how that works.

I got exactly what I wanted, and I became exactly who I asked myself to become. I helped increase the income of all of my clients by multiples – I hired great people, helping them earn great, high-paying jobs.

I was just a dude – albeit, with a lot of money.

I had no plan, and no clue.

I had no identity.

I had everything and nothing, all at once.

Just like a ship without a captain – my company hit an iceberg and started to sink. Fast. When one of our clients (a billion dollar company that went belly up because of some shady business at the executive levels) – the income of the company that I had built went from $35k+ / month to about $12k.

Then, my other clients – for one reason or another – started dropping out like flies. It wasn't because we weren't providing the service. In fact, we were doing such a good job – that they were set up for success – with or without us.

It was the damndest thing. All of them were happy – yet they were all jumping ship at the same time.

No new clients were coming in.

Then, just like that we somehow finished the job for my first client (the $10k a month one) and he no longer needed us either. In the span of exactly 3 weeks, I went from making more money than I'd ever dreamed possible to less money than I was making waiting tables.

What.

The.

FUCK?

I honestly thought that I wasn't deserving of all this money. I wasn't deserving of all this success. The life around me that I had created was foreign to me, unfamiliar, distant, and not real.

Just like that, everything collapsed.

I had no employees. I had no income. I had no hope.

I had no company.

I had completely failed, or so I thought at the time. My self-worth and net-worth fell to an all-time low. I started eating a lot of bad food, not exercising, and doing anything I could to take my mind off of reality.

I was alienating myself from friends, from family – from life.

Thankfully , through it all I have been blessed with an amazing wife who believed in me. She wasn't without her own moments of weakness and doubts – but she believed in me. She knew I would find a way back up.

Much like I believe in YOU, I know that you will find a way to your own personal success.

Through a lot of hard work and a lot of soul-searching – we're now recovering at a healthy, steady pace.

We once again have a mountain of debt – but this time it's different. This time I know what needs to be done, I know how to do it, and I'm motivated to make it happen.

This time, there will be no self-sabotage.

There will only be learning, growing, and success.

There will be mistakes that are made, I'm sure, but I will view them as allies instead of enemies. Every mistake I make is one step closer to success.

Every mistake I have already made, is another reason I'm advancing so much more quickly this time around.

It's funny y'know…

We're living on 20 acres in southern California, own 4 horses, 2 dogs, and a cat – and are happily married. We live a damn good life and travel whenever we're so inclined. We eat better than we ever have. We're healthier and more fit that we've ever been.

In the eyes of most – we already have success. We do, I whole-heartedly believe this – yet we still want more. We have more to give – and therefore, more to strive for.

One thing that I've had to deal with in the time since the downfall of my consultancy – is my own self-image.

I've had to reimagine myself from who I once was.

If I wanted to be successful, wealthy, and happy – then I needed to align who I was with those goals.

I had to find out who "I" was.

I'd given up on my dreams of music, and acting, and expressing myself through any creative means. These were my lifelong dreams – and I was abandoning them like an orphaned child. I was paying for this betrayal of self in more ways than I could count.

I still saw myself as a struggling artist, who would forsake himself for the good of those around him. That's exactly what I did, the problem is it caught up with me much faster than I ever thought it would.

"Take care of yourself, and you'll always be in a better position to help those around you."

The nice thing about self-image is that you can choose each and every detail about it. Nobody else can have the final say.

As such, I would eventually learn to redesign myself as an up and coming artist and entrepreneur. A healthy, & happy individual – not afraid of speaking my mind, a person who always did the right thing, I am a loving husband, a leader, and a good man. I care about people, but do not care what they think about me.

In the last year I've redefined that self-image one further step – I no longer refer to myself as 'up and coming', as I realized THAT in and of itself is a quasi-negative.

Now, I define myself as this:

I am a successful and creative artist and entrepreneur. I am healthy, and I am happy. I speak my mind and live without fear. I do the right thing; I am a loving husband, leader – and will live my life to be remembered as a great man. I care about people, yet do not let what others say about me, or think about me bring this self-image down.

As a seemingly direct result of thinking in such a positive and directing way – you end up living in accordance and in harmony with these thoughts. Your words convey your self-worth, and your actions portray each and every word. You no longer betray your thoughts, your ID, or yourself.

You too can achieve the same fast-tracked results, and you can avoid a downfall like I had to experience. First however, you need to get out the laptop or a good ole' fashioned pen and paper.

Start by going back to what you wrote down earlier and writing down the words that describe who you want to become. If you can't think of any, try thinking of the things you DO NOT want to become (this is a trick to help get the creative juices flowing). Don't write down negatives – instead, write down their antonyms.

If you don't want to be **bad** – then be *what?*

If you don't want to be **sad** – then be *what?*

Imagine everything that you possibly want. Decide each and every aspect of your life from here on out. Don't leave anything out. Don't focus solely on monetary success – or you'll end up suffering the same fate I had to recover from.

How would you describe 'future you'? How would others describe 'future you'? Where does 'future you' live? What does 'future you' spend your time doing? What makes 'future you' happy? What will 'future you' not stand for? What will 'future you' fight for?

Think in terms of specifics. Think in terms of adjectives – highly detailed descriptions. The more detail, the better. Think about your mental state, your physical state, your emotional state, your logical state, and your spiritual state.

How do you fulfill all of your needs? From the most basic to the most existential of needs – if you make a game plan now your future will go a lot more smoothly.

It's a lot easier to get somewhere when you have a map, isn't it?

As for the question that almost nobody seems to like to answer – "who am I now?" – realize that this isn't that important. Your past does not dictate your future. The 'present' is constantly over – if you think about it, you are living in the future. You will never get 10 years ago, 1 year ago, 6 months ago, 20 minutes ago, or even 1 split-second ago back. Deal with it. Embrace it.

The self-worth and the person you have become have not previously been intentional creations. They have been manipulated and disfigured by everyone and everything you have encountered in life – a byproduct of your environment.

Step out of who you are, or rather who you've been - decide now that you are exactly who you want to be.

Start being 'future you' and let the future become now.

You'll start living up to the expectations of that image. Trust me, it's happened for me and I've seen it happen for my clients.

Just know that if you stumble, and when you fall that is perfectly okay – nobody is perfect.

What is important is that you don't let that stop you. Don't let failure hold you back.

Failure is simply a sign that you are trying to succeed. It's not a negative – it is a positive. Analyze what went wrong, as well as how to not let that happen again – and move on.

Get off the couch and take one step. By doing this, the honest truth is: you're already further ahead than the majority who never bothered to get their butts off the couch in the first place.

Be the best you that you can be, starting right now. Leave who you have been, and who you have become, thus far - behind you. Learn from your mistakes, modify your direction, and take that first step into the "you" that you deserve to be.

Become the "you" that this world so desperately needs.

Become the "you" that you know – you are meant to be.

Become 'future you'.

Become you.

IV

REVERSE POLARITY

"Once you replace negative thoughts
with positive ones, you'll start having positive results."
- Willie Nelson

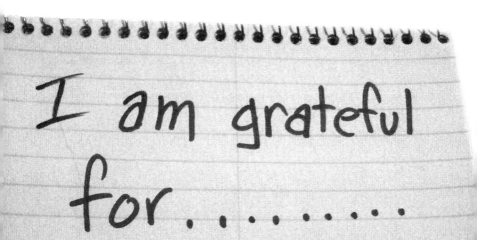

Reverse Polarity

Picture this.

You want success so badly, that it's all you can think about. It eats at you, from the moment you wake up to the last second before you drift off to sleep at night.

The people around you just don't understand though… They're very negative every time you speak about your goals, your ambitions, and your desire for change.

They say, "What??? Are you too good for us now?"

"You can't do that…"

"You're not smart enough!"

"You're not good enough!" they repeat over and over – the words differ, but the message is always the same. A million reasons why you can't get what you want. A million excuses as to why they've given up. A million anchors tie you to the port of miserable failure.

It's comfortable there, because it's where most people stay.

Sometimes, negativity isn't even overt. It's more of a 'lack of positivity'. There is no sense in wasting your time away playing video games instead of engaging in the game of life. There's nothing wrong with things like games or television when enjoyed in moderation – but when they start taking up a predominant portion of your life – it may be time to re-evaluate.

Remember, misery loves company; excuses multiply in groups of underachievers. They never took their chances. They never believed in themselves. As a result – they want you to join them – or at the very least they sure as heck don't want you to leave them there alone.

My life was just like this, for a very long time. I was miserable, and I had very little money. I wanted to move to the United States (from Canada) and pursue my dreams of becoming a performer / entertainer.

I was working a job as a delivery driver. That job didn't pay very well, but it was easy and lacked responsibility. Looking back, I was simply fulfilling my obligations to society by having a job. I did the least amount possible because it wasn't what I wanted – but I didn't want to disappoint anyone.

One day, I realized that without deciding to seize the day – and deciding to remove myself from such a negative world – my life would NEVER get better. I would get more depressed. I would hate life more and more.

I saved up for a few weeks, and bought a 1984 Dodge Caravan minivan. It was the perfect vehicle for packing up all of my crap and leaving town.

That's just what I did. Every belonging I had was thrown into the van, and I was on my way to Washington State. I found out on my trip that this van had a tiny pinhole leak in the gas tank. As such, it spit gas on the road as I drove.

Most would likely find this a great excuse to quit, or to postpone. Not me. Not this time. It wasn't exactly safe, but it suited its purpose. It got me one step closer, while simultaneously burning the bridge to return home.

I made it to Washington. I was on my way.

By simply removing myself from negativity, I was one step closer to living my dreams, actually enjoying my life, and being the person that I was meant to be.

Soon enough, though – like everyone who leaves their problems behind without a plan set in front of them… I fell back into similar patterns. I found myself surrounded once more by negative people, negative situations, and carrying around a negative mindset.

What I didn't realize at the time was this:

Simply removing yourself from negativity is not enough. Negativity needs to be replaced by positivity – otherwise it creates a vacuum that attracts the negativity back in full force.

Negativity exists in a few different forms & patterns. There are negative situations, negative relationships, and negative words, thoughts, and actions.

If you can remove enough of these negative patterns and replace them with positive forms – you will see massive change in your life.

By focusing on positive patterns, the negative ones will fall behind you – as long as you keep moving forward.

Focusing on the negative patterns will generally 'keep you in the shit'. So do not focus on your negative patterns, instead train yourself to recognize them – and when they happen – replace them with positive ones.

Find positive peers. Remove the ones that are holding you back.

Find positive surroundings. Listen to uplifting music. Read uplifting books. Watch uplifting videos and movies. Learn skills. Gain confidence.

Speak positively.

Think positively.

Act with confidence. Be awesome to people. Be awesome to yourself.

"You are the average of the five people you spend the most time with." - Jim Rohn

The people that we hang around influence us, both directly and indirectly. We pick up similar speech patterns and slang, we often share their hobbies and habits, and generally our moods reflect our nearest companions.

Unfortunately, because most people don't make conscious decisions – their friends / social circle are comprised of people who they picked up by proximity. Meaning – the people who are around us most often, become our friends. It's not based on merit, or any positive criteria whatsoever, but instead it's based solely on the fact that it was convenient to hang around with that person.

Is your social circle one you chose because it helps you further your goals?

Do they have your back when times get tough?

Do the people you surround yourself with help you further your goals, support you, and care about your needs and desires?

If you're answering yes, then congratulations – you are one of a small percentage. If, however, you find yourself answering 'no', like most people – then perhaps it's time to sit back for a minute...

Stop being busy for a little bit. Realize that everything will still be here tomorrow, and if it's not, that's okay – new opportunities will arise soon.

It's vital to take a few minutes to look at your surroundings – only then can you truly begin to interpret reality as it truly is, and start to become fully self-aware.

Self-awareness combined with consistent action will get you nearly anything you can set your mind to. It is exactly how world records are broken; and it's how breakthroughs are discovered. Understand that this is how excellence is achieved.

Find friends with similar interests to the ones you wish to pursue. Find people who are further ahead than you. Surround yourself with people who have what you want.

You would be absolutely surprised at how much simply surrounding yourself with the right people can absolutely change your life.

It is critical to note, however, that you can't just surround yourself with these people – you need to take note of what they're doing, and if you don't understand why they do what they do – ask them. Understand the actions that lead to their success – to your DESIRED success, and then repeat them. It's more than mindset, it's more than personality – it's about learning to master the same skills as these people. Do this, and you will win.

The more value you give to the world, the more you will receive.

Once you follow this advice, you will have positive role models that will improve the quality of your life in countless ways.

You will be surrounded by positive people – which will place you in positive situations.

By being immersed in this positive new demi-culture, and by making consistent, conscious decisions to improve yourself – your thoughts, your words, and your actions will become positive – and you will be one step closer to the life that you desire.

If you don't know any people who have what you want, or are looking to become what you want to be – there are many places to find them.

Use your resourcefulness to find them.

You can use the internet to find meet-up groups, forums, and get-togethers.

Think of where these people would hang out. Go there. Meet people.

If you don't know how to effectively meet people and make them like you, then I highly suggest reading "How to Win Friends and Influence People" by Dale Carnegie. That book will set you in the right direction for communicating, meeting, and engaging with people.

Find tools, resources, people, situations, events, courses and music that make you feel better, help you to achieve more, and finally - strive to achieve your own personal success.

I can't tell you what your own personal success should be – you have to discover that for yourself.

This is your "why", this is your story.

This is for you to discover and use as your strength through the bad times. Use your "why" as a light in dark times.

If you need help on learning how to uncover your 'why' – check out my book on the topic over at **readshanehunter.com/why**

Keep your eyes on the prize.

What if you take every negative thought, and self-doubt that you ever have – and you flip it into a positive?

What power would that have on your life?

Picture yourself in a boxing match.

You've just been knocked down by a very powerful punch.

The ref is counting... 1, 2, 3...

You know that you have until the 10 count to get to your feet.

4...

5...

6...

Your significant other is ringside cheering you on, all of your loved ones, your mentors, your fans – they're all cheering your name.

Man... That ground sure feels nice right now... A helluva lot better than getting punched even one more time by this glove-wearing animal that you're fighting...

But you've worked your whole life to earn that championship belt; you've worked your ass off for this fight – to win. You've given your all; you've given everything to advance your dreams.

If you let that ref count to 10, you may never fight again. You may never get a chance at the championship belt again. You will lose your dreams. You will lose everything that you've worked for.

Are you really willing to give ALL that up, in one moment of weakness?

Do you stay down, or do you get up?

You tell yourself to get up.

You know exactly how to get up – you've practiced it seemingly millions of times...

7...

You summon your will.

You summon your desire and your courage.

You get up.

The fight carries on, and you go blow for blow with the most difficult adversary you've ever done battle with. You're both bloodied and bruised.

But you both know; only one of you goes home tonight the winner.

The other goes home without the win, without the prize, without everything you've worked so very hard for...

You fight the rest of that fight, and you WIN dammit!

Don't win because it's easy.

Win it because it is HARD – it's the hardest thing you've ever done.

You've never put so much effort into anything.

You've wanted this your whole life, and you've fought a long hard battle to get it.

Giving up now would be cheating yourself.

Don't you give up – success is almost yours. So what are you going to do about it?

You KNOW that failure is not an option. Not this time. Not with this goal.

Success is yours, if you just reach out, and take it.

If you don't defeat yourself, it is highly unlikely that anybody else will ever be able to do so.

This is the mindset of a champion.

This is the inner dialogue of your greatest heroes.

This is the story of the winner.

This is your story.

Now, perhaps you are thinking...

Shane, I have tried doing all this. I've given my best, I've trained my booty off, and I've faced my demons and my challenges head on...

I've fallen. I've got back up.

Only to be embarrassingly knocked down, yet again...

Remember earlier, when I was talking about experiencing disappointment, and my failure?

To create success, I got back up after my fights – and I watched the metaphorical "film footage" of the battle. I analyzed just where I went wrong.

Then I went on to create a faster, stronger, smarter, better version of myself.

I trained harder, I learned more, I took bigger, yet more calculated risks. I created a better 'me'.

As a result? I won the next battle, and I won the war.

Just like you are going to do.

V

HOW CAN I?

"Ask, and you will receive;
seek, and you will find;
knock, and the door will be opened to you."
- Matthew 7:7

How Can I?

What do you think would happen if you replaced every time you think or say "I can't" with "How Can I?"

From my own personal experience, I can tell you – beyond a shadow of a doubt that you will become more successful, happier, and achieve more than you ever thought possible.

There is power in the question.

Question everything.

Every time you have a negative thought, or say something negative to yourself, or someone else – change that negativity into a positive, ambitious question.

"I can't" becomes, "How can I?"

"That's impossible!" becomes, "How can I make this possible?"

"I don't like this / I hate this" becomes, "How can I learn to enjoy or like this?"

"Man, I really fucked up! I'm such a failure" becomes, "Well... At least I can learn something from this. What CAN I learn from this?"

Imagine if there were no limits - only limitless possibilities.

The nice thing about asking questions is – you don't need to imagine a limitless, infinite universe.

By simply asking more questions of yourself and of your world - you step into an abundant universe left with no alternative but to deliver the answers that you seek.

Questions are much too powerful to ONLY be used as a simple reframing tool. When you start to use questions daily, you will open yourself to all sorts of new experiences, learning, and opportunities.

When you replace "I don't know how" with "How can I learn more about this?" you open yourself up to a whole new world of understanding, wisdom, and mastery.

We live in an age that is unlike any before it. We have all of the common information available at our fingertips. We can access it via home computer, laptop, smart phone, and even smart watches.

We can access this information in the shower, at the coffee shop, or even while travelling.

You have questions – and the world has answers. For the first time ever, you have access to the entire world. You can access information from anywhere, in many forms, at nearly any location of your choosing.

Once you start looking for answers, the avalanche happens and you start learning at a seemingly exponential rate. You will get smarter, you will develop new skills, you will get better, you will get stronger, and you will become more successful.

Now, this doesn't mean go out and absorb everything like a dry sponge in sewer water. Listen to your inner voice, trust your intuition, and be careful where you gather your knowledge from.

All I'm saying is, be careful about where you get your information from. Always check multiple sources to see if the information is both accurate and up to date.

Some questions that I've asked myself over the past decade that you may consider asking yourself are:

- Am I learning what I need to know to make my dreams a reality?
- How can I learn faster?
- How can I retain more knowledge and information?
- What skills do I need to master, in order to accomplish my goals?
- Is it faster for me to do this, or to outsource it?
- How can I give more value to the world?
- How can I make more money than I am now, while working the same amount or less?
- What scares me, and how can I learn more about it so that I no longer fear it?

- What do I love doing? How can I do more of it?
- What do I hate doing? How can I not hate it as much, or how can I do less of it?

I ask many more questions in addition to these ones – but this is just a short list of questions to prompt you into asking your own. It took me years to understand the value in these questions and their respective answers – years that are now yours to leverage. Enjoy!

Now go, start asking questions, and maybe even get yourself some answers.

VI

STATE MANAGEMENT

"You have power over your mind – not outside events. Realize this, and you will find strength."

- Marcus Aurelius

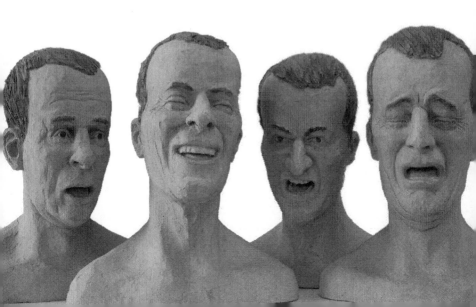

State Management

You cannot control external circumstances, the way people treat you, or the way that people talk to you.

What you CAN change is the way that you respond to these external forces.

When you allow external forces to bother you, to bring you down, to hurt your feelings, or to stop you from pursuing your dreams and goals – you are making a subconscious decision.

You are making the choice to allow these external forces to manipulate you. If you feel like your response is out of your control and chosen by anyone other than yourself – this simply means that you're making the choice to NOT make a choice. You are making the choice to feel helpless and out of control.

Empower yourself, and make the decision to not allow these external forces, stories, circumstances, and interactions to negatively affect you.

Take a deep breath, and realize that most people function on a completely subconscious and reactionary plane. They are not empowered – they are simply reacting. They are not making the decision to treat you this way; they are simply reacting to external forces that they didn't take ownership over. They are letting their weakness spill over onto you. You have the choice to stop the cycle.

You can rise above this negativity by acknowledging that it's possible, and realizing that controlling your reaction – is the only thing that is real. It's the only thing that you can directly change.

Wake up and smell the reactions.

This concept will take some time for you to master and will be difficult for the untrained mind.

The good news is – the more you practice it, the easier it gets.

You should know that there are some physiological tricks that you can use to balance your state management. When you learn them, it's actually pretty dang cool.

For example – excercising plays a dramatic role in both your emotional health, as well as your physical wellness. There are a lot of chemicals released when you work out that you otherwise would never get. These chemicals help to balance your emotions and stress levels.

You don't need to run out and get a gym membership right now (though I do highly recommend it). Just try going for a walk a few times a week. Maybe 20 minutes, hell – 5 minutes for the first few times if you're really struggling and aren't really the 'move around' type. Just do something, and you'll start to see results.

I know this works miracles, as I've personally gone from 43% fat to 16% fat in the last year and a half. The difference is INSANELY GOOD. I feel more alive, I feel more like me.

I feel less trapped, and far more empowered. I think you will too.

Aside from exercise, try monitoring yourself when you're experiencing various emotions.

The next time you find yourself feeling any particular emotion – I want you to take note of your body language.

Your physiology is a powerful tool.

When you are sad, you'll likely notice a slumped posture, droopy shoulders and face, maybe a frown.

When you are pissed off, you'll likely notice that you are extremely tense. Clenched fists, tight shoulders, a tight neck, a scowl on your face, and maybe grinding teeth?

When you are happy, how often do you look like either of these examples?

Not very often, I'd hazard to guess...

After you've taken notice of the state of your body in these various moods – I want you to try something out with me...

I want you to take the body language that you noted from your happy, joyful, and content states and consciously manipulate your body so that you are mimicking those same positions.

Try smiling. Put your shoulders back. Puff up your chest. Take deep, fulfilling breaths in through your nose, and out through your mouth. Make your eyes wide and happy. Stand up with your back straight.

If you're really down, look up and crack the biggest, most goofy grin that you can possibly muster – show those teeth!

Think about funny stuff, or stuff that makes you happy. Think of your favorite joke, your favorite scene your favorite movie, a line from your favorite song... Picture it in your mind's eye. Close your eyes if you need to, in order to picture it. Hear it. Feel it.

Maintain this position, this feeling, and this state for at LEAST a minute or two. (It's okay to shift your mind to different **positive** things – you don't have to focus on the same joke...)

Once you've done this, ask yourself, "What's happening? Do I feel any different?"

Let me guess? You ARE starting to feel different?

You're either going to giggle and snicker, or at the very least start feeling a teeny-tiny bit better. You may think it's because you feel stupid – but what is happening is your physiology is working against your current mood.

When your body language and mental imagery say something, your mind will generally follow suit – whether 'grumpy you' likes it or not.

Enjoy your newfound superpower. Use it frequently, and notice the difference.

VII

THE FINAL FIGHT

"Impossible is just a big word thrown around by small men
who find it easier to live in the world they've been given
than to explore the power they have to change it.
Impossible is not a fact. It's an opinion.
Impossible is not a declaration. It's a dare.
Impossible is potential.
Impossible is temporary.
Impossible is nothing."

- Muhammed Ali

The Final Fight

Welcome to the most important chapter of this book. Without this concept, everything else you've just read becomes pointless.

This is the step where many promising 'up-and-comers' fall by the wayside.

You know the type – those that seem like they have everything figured out. Then, like a rock they plummet from greatness back into the abyss of failure and self-loathing.

Why do they fall? They've done ALL the work, they've gone through ALL the motions, they've worked their butts off – and yet, they believe they've failed and they feel defeated. Why?

These would-be heroes fail because they decide one day to fight The Final Fight. They decide that this is their 'last stand', and it's now or never, all or nothing.

If they succeed, everything is awesome – it's business as usual, and they're onto the next challenge.

If they fail, they pack their stuff up and go home sobbing that something wasn't fair, or they gave it their best and got so close, but no cigar. They decide they're done. There is no more getting up.

If you decide to NEVER fight The Final Fight – then you cannot fail.

Sure, you can lose the battle – but the war is yours for the taking. Simple persistence will beat a large majority of the folks out there who claim they want the same prize that you want.

When you lose a battle, learn from it. Realize that the war is far from over. At the very worst, let stumbling on this obstacle make you realize that you are making forward progress.

When you understand and apply the concepts of this book, and you refuse to fight The Final Fight – you are set up for success.

Complete and total success.

Think about the Sylvester Stallone movie "Rocky". He wasn't the strongest, he wasn't the most talented, but he wasn't a quitter either. Through steadfast perseverance, he transformed himself into a champion. He accomplished his goals. He achieved greatness, by simply refusing to stay down. He refused to give up.

He took a LOT of hits. It wasn't pretty. It wasn't easy.

Yet, Rocky refused to fight The Final Fight.

Do not tie your happiness to success or to winning each and every battle. Instead, learn from every experience and continue on the march towards what you want from life. Tie your happiness to your effort. Tie yourself emotionally to the fact that you are strong, you are courageous, and you will not give up. Get back up.

As time passes, and you attempt to approach your dreams – you will realize that your dreams are a living, breathing, organic thing. They are not static. Dreams are ever changing, and constantly evolving.

Sometimes not hitting your goals or achieving success can be the best thing that will ever happen to you.

Pursuing these temporary dreams still gets you much closer to your real dreams. Pursuit gets you closer to who you want to be, as well as to where you want to be.

If you remove the negativity and use intelligent, positive, ambitious questions – sometimes failure will be your biggest achievements, your best lessons, and your most fulfilling rewards.

This only holds true if you refuse to ever fight The Final Fight. Don't give up, don't give in. Keep moving forward.

As a quick review – your keys to success are as follows:

1. Remove the need for external permission and validation / Grant yourself universal permission and validation from this point forward.
2. Define your own self-image. Discover who you are and transform that person into who you want to be.
3. Remove negativity from your life, and replace it with positivity.
4. Ask empowering, ambitious questions of yourself.
5. Manage your emotional state & choose your reactions.
6. Never fight The Final Fight. Never give up. Never surrender.

When you follow these 6 steps, you will win.

Every. Single. Time.

I'd really love to hear what your plans are, now that you've read this book. What are you going to do now that you know these concepts and strategies?

Come like my Facebook page here: **readshanehunter.com/fb**

I'd love for you to come and post your stories, your comments, or any questions you may have for me there. I look forward to talking with you, and helping you along with your journey! Keep an eye out for emails from me.

If you somehow didn't end up on my email list, you can go sign up for it by going to **readshanehunter.com/reader** and entering your name and email in that form.

I purposely end this book in an abrupt fashion, with no real closure or motivational ass kickings like your typical self-help book.

The idea is, I want to leave you wanting more. I want you to go forth and apply what you've read here. Take action.

I do this, because I want YOU to decide your future. I cannot tell you what you need to do. I can only give you the methods, and the tools you need to get there.

Decide your fate. Decide your future. **Decide.**

"I am the master of my fate, I am the captain of my soul." - Invictus, by William Ernest Henley

NOTES

NOTES

NOTES

NOTES

NOTES

NOTES

NOTES

NOTES

NOTES

25889809R00076

Printed in Poland
by Amazon Fulfillment
Poland Sp. z o.o., Wrocław